DARK SWANS AND PAINTED FACES

DARK SWANS AND PAINTED FACES

A TALE OF THE VIETNAM WAR

Finalist in the 2013 William Faulkner-William Wisdom Creative Writing Competition

JOHN SCHALESTOCK

ISBN: 978-1-947825-60-4
Dark Swans and Painted Faces
Copyright © 2014 by John Schalestock

All rights reserved.

No part of this publication may be reproduced, distributed, or transmitted in any form or by any means, including photocopying, recording, or other electronic or mechanical methods, without the prior written permission of the publisher, except in the case of brief quotations embodied in critical reviews and certain other noncommercial uses permitted by copyright law.

For permission requests, write to the publisher at the address below.

Yorkshire Publishing
3207 South Norwood Avenue
Tulsa, Oklahoma 74135
www.YorkshirePublishing.com
918.394.2665

DEDICATION

This book is dedicated to all the Force Recon Marines and their Navy corpsmen who never returned from those dark and lonely places. Semper Fidelis.

And to my wife Anne who has kept the faith.

ACKNOWLEDGEMENTS

The author would like to thank Lana Lee Barrett Owens, old friend and fellow writer, whose insights, suggestions and encouragement made this book possible.

SPIKE TEAM RODENT

In the summer of 1964, on a day that never was, somewhere in the trackless jungle of northern Laos near the border of North Vietnam, a Marine Force Recon team is on the run.

It is the night of the third day and they are desperately tired. Only their training and superb physical fitness has kept them going. That and the knowledge that they are on their own and that the CIA and Lyndon Johnson who have put them here would vehemently deny their mission, or that they even existed.

Of the seven man team, three have been hit and their leader, Captain Kevin O'Bannion, is worried about the blood trails they may be leaving. He knows they are being tracked by an NVA hunter-killer team bent on revenge. And he knows that the North Vietnamese are relentless and dedicated and there are too many of them for the team to take on even in an ambush.

So they push southward, hoping to reach an extraction point where an Air America King Bee H-34 helicopter may (or as they all concede) may not pick them up. But for now it is their only hope.

They have discarded everything they can spare and carry only their M-14 rifles and 10 extra magazines of ammo and 3 canteens of water. The team's sniper, Billy Ray Wallace, has placed a condom over the muzzle of his Remington 700 bolt action rifle and has smeared extra oil on the bolt but he has discarded its sheepskin scabbard and carries the rifle slung over his shoulder with his thumb holding the sling outward ready for immediate action. He has also removed the lens caps from the 3 x 9 power Redfield scope and the rifle has a 30/06 boat tail match grade round in the chamber.

The M-14s are new and impressive weapons but at eleven pounds they are not light to carry. Their twenty round magazines are loaded with 7.62 millimeter 160 grain full metal jacketed rounds which are not light either but in the bush are worth their weight in gold. The heavy slugs, moving at 2800 feet per second can easily blow through underbrush and foliage and are not easily deflected.

The M-14s also have a selector lever that allows the shooter to switch from single fire to fully automatic. But this burns ammo at 700 rounds a minute so it is used only as an immediate reaction response when ambushed.

Only Gunnery Sergeant Robottom carries what these young Marines consider an antique—a Thompson submachine gun. And only he knows for sure just how good this weapon is in close combat. He knows its heavy .45 caliber slugs will blow through dense vegetation like it was cotton candy and leave severe punishment where they strike.

Robottom had been one of the fabled Marine Raiders in the Pacific War twenty years before and he has utmost faith in this weapon and knows it intimately. With its muzzle compensator that keeps the barrel from rising under fire, Robottom is deadly accurate with it even when firing at the high cyclic rate of 800 rounds a minute. And he doesn't mind carrying the dozen extra 20 round magazines of .45 ammo that the weapon uses. The ammo also fits the .45 caliber pistol he carries on the web belt around his waist and he has a bag of extra loose rounds in his rucksack.

Like most combat veterans Robottom is under no illusions. When the team had been training in Thailand they had run into a platoon of Pathet Lao insurgents and routed them after a short firefight. It was for Jack, the young radio operator, his first time under fire and he was exuberant after it was over and that none of the team had been hit.

"We're just too bad for these motherfuckers" he had exalted.

Gunny Robottom had grabbed him by the collar and put his mouth next to his ear like he was about to tell him a terrible secret.

"Today was our day Marine" he had hissed. That don't mean tomorrow will be. When you go into combat, you give yourself up as a dead man. You'll fight better that way. You just remember that."

He was sure right about that Jack remembers as he carefully squashes a bug that has been crawling across his blood soaked bandage. Too fucking right.

The team has loaded a tracer every third round in their M-14 magazines. These are valuable in a close firefight because there is usually no time for looking through the rifles sights and squeezing off rounds so the ability to see where the rounds are actually going is of great value.

Gunny Robottom has had their 7.62 tracer ammo reloaded by his old friend Gunny Charlie Dan, 2nd Force Recon's armorer at Camp Lejeune in North Carolina. Dan has replaced the standard strontium salts and magnesium perchlorate that burns red and notifies the enemy that they are being shot at by Americans with barium salts that makes the tracers burn green—just like the enemy's AK-47.

Gunny Dan had also modified the M-14's flash suppressor by welding over the bottom vents. The escaping gases from the top vents pushed the muzzle down and reduced the weapon's tendency to rise when firing in the full auto mode. The outgoing rounds of the M-14 don't sound exactly the same as an AK-47 but close enough to confuse the enemy who mostly only see the color of the tracers going over anyway. And in combat, a moment of confusion can be a light year of grace.

The men have stuffed C rations into their pockets but they feel little hunger now and continue to run on the ragged engine of fading adrenalin and the green and white amphetamine pills which they use sparingly. Thirst has become their first circle of hell and their remaining equipment, minimal though it is, is brutally heavy in the hot, humid air.

Their camouflage suits are the same ones used by the Marine Raiders of WW2 that Gunny Robotom had liberated from a dusty warehouse at Camp Lejeune. He has sterilized them of any markings that would indicate their origin before handing them out to the team. In the years to come, even the Army's Green Berets, and the hard core SOG recon teams will admire and trade for these old suits that blend better with their surroundings than their own modern, tiger striped versions.

Now the suits are blackened from sweat and dried blood and the brims of their camouflaged boonie hats droop like sodden wreaths around their heads. The uniforms chafe against their bodies like a cruel second skin and the canteens have left bruises where they have banged against the wet cloth. But the Marines know that the water and ammo are all that stands between them and death and there is no thought of leaving any of it.

The wounded are suffering badly and the team must stop to rest more often than O'Bannion would like. O'Bannion himself has taken a grazing round from an AK-47 across his forehead and the green combat dressing wrapped around his head is soaked with blood that has turned black in the stifling heat.

O'Bannion was a former All American linebacker from Notre Dame with a face that Knute Rockne would have recognized and a true Irish tenor voice that is so pure he can be forgiven for using it to seduce women. It is a precious gift from his Irish grandfather and he knows it.

But now, in this dark corner of the world, beneath the camouflage paint and blackened cordite and the sweat and smell of their own unwashed bodies, tiny blood trails from his wound have etched themselves against his forehead and his handsome Irish face is dominated by green eyes that have become hard and unforgiving and seem to change from green to gray to black in brief heartbeats.

Behind him, Corporal Jack Phillips, the team's radio operator, tries to take a deep breath to control his breathing but the shrapnel wound in his shoulder is throbbing and the straps of the radio on his back burns like a branding iron. His battle dressing has bled through and the blood has turned his camouflage jacket black and Jack can smell the sulfa powder that their Navy corpsman, Doc Walker had sprinkled over it.

His left arm is strapped across his chest beneath a sheathed Ka-Bar fighting knife that is taped hilt down just above his wounded arm. Jack carries his M-14 slung across his right shoulder but he also has an automatic Colt .45 pistol strapped to his right leg and its worn black holster is secured against his thigh with rawhide thongs. He doesn't notice the pistol's weight and even if he had he wouldn't be without it and the four extra magazines of ammo strapped to his belt.

The pistol has already saved his life on this mission and its seven round magazine is full of heavy, .45 caliber rounds and there is an eighth round in the chamber. The 230 grain slugs will knock a man off his feet no matter where he is hit. Jack knows this is a good thing for the shooter.

Jack's radio is a Korean War vintage AN/GRC-9 (Angry Nine the radio operators called it) that had been used by the heroic radio operators of Chesty Puller's Marines at the Chosin Reservoir who had sat back to back, operating their radios and firing their Colt .45 pistols at the oncoming Chinese until they were overrun. Jack is carrying it because their mission is so sensitive it has been decided to use the radio only in its Morse code mode, sending five letter groups to maintain the mission's secrecy.

When Jack had cleaned and tuned the radio he saw an inscription scratched inside the waterproof cover. It had read, "Smitty" and the words "FOX CO. 2/7. CHOSIN RESERVOIR 1950" and then in bolder strokes, "Semper Fi."

Jack, like all Marines, knew the history of the "Frozen Chosin" where the First Marine Division, cut off and surrounded, had fought their way to the sea taking their dead and wounded with them and mauling eight Chinese communist divisions so badly they never saw action again during the war. And where the Marines had been awarded five Medals of Honor and a dozen Navy Crosses.

Jack had looked at the inscription with reverence. "Semper Fi my brother," he thought to himself. "Fox company! Shit! The skipper would have been Captain Barber, one of the Medal of Honor winners". Then he thought…"wonder if Smitty made it out?" Jack had seen the deep gouges in the cover that looked like they had been caused by shrapnel. "Wish this radio could talk" Jack thought. It already seemed like a comrade.

The radio consisted of a backpack transceiver, an antenna pack and a hand cranked generator. The load was usually divided between three men but Jack has discarded everything except the long wire antenna and given it to the man carrying the generator. He keeps the flimsy sectioned whip antenna and straps it down behind the radio on his back to clear the overhanging branches.

The radio is rugged and powerful but it weighs twenty nine pounds. Jack is carrying it because it is powerful enough to send Morse Code at a long, penetrating wavelength and Jack has learned to mimic the fists of the North Vietnamese radio operators who use a lot of Morse Code in their communications and the code gives some security protection in the CW mode because only the carrier is turned on and off and the NVA radio direction finders have a harder time zeroing in on it. At least that is Jack's theory. Now he's not so sure.

The Angry Nine is their only link with the outside world and its maximum range during the day is only about 30 miles. In daylight it was useful only because the special ops aircraft carried an airborne version that could relay the ground transmissions hundreds of miles.

It has three frequency bands from two to twelve megahertz and can be operated either in voice or Morse code (CW) mode. But at night, a good radio operator using the lower frequencies could work the ionosphereic skip and reach all the way back to Udorn if the conditions were right.

Still the weight of the angry nine's generator is a brutal tradeoff and the man carrying it curses all radio operators.

FALLBACK

In the night the team has paused to rest beside a dark mountain stream that slithers past them in the moonlight like a glittering snake and O'Bannion signals them down to the water's edge where they rest their backs against the muddy bank. The water is cool in the humid air and a night mist floats like a ghostly shroud above the dark flowing surface.

The men fill their canteens and pour it over their heads before dropping halazone tablets in them and drinking the cool dark water. Then O'Bannion points to his feet and signals half of the team to take off their boots and soak their feet in the flowing water.

Those watching the trail pretend they don't hear the quiet splash of healing water on blistered feet. They face outward, over the bank with their rifles pointed towards the darkness and will hold the line until it is their turn at the healing river. They watch intently and their discipline would have made the Spartans at Thermopylae nod in approval.

Billy Ray faces to the rear and rests his rifle across the bank and peers intently into the dark shadows behind them. He can kill at a thousand yards with the bolt rifle but now, even fifty yards is a gift to be hoped for.

Without turning he pours his canteen on the back of his neck and the water feels wonderful as it flows down onto his sweat soaked back. Charlie Dumas, his spotter, takes the Starlight night scope out of his rucksack and mounts it on his M-14 and scans the darkness. He looks at Billy Ray and shakes his head. Nothing.

After the team has drunk and soaked their feet and have stored the pleasure of these things like treasures in their minds, they clean their rifles, two men at a time.

They release the magazines and cup their hands over the bolt to muffle the sound and pull back the operating rod and eject the round in the chamber and catch it with their free hand. Then they run a cleaning rod down the barrel and wipe the open receiver with an oily rag.

Before the firefight the weapons had been spotless but now they are blackened with cordite and the hot, ever present moisture has already begun its rusty work on the exposed metal of the chamber mouth.

Yet the weapon's proper functioning is life and death to the Marines and they know it and they clean their rifles with a religious commitment.

When they finish, they strip the ammo from the magazines and wipe each round and then carefully reload them. The tracer rounds have been tipped in green by Gunny Dan to remind them of what they are and the Marines carefully stagger them every third round. Then they tuck their armpits over the open receivers to muffle the sound of retracting bolts and ejecting rounds and ease the magazines back into the bottom of their rifles, flip the safety on and release the bolt and ease it forward. The bolt picks up a round from the magazine and chambers it and it locks with a metallic click.

Then they lie back against the river bank and rest.

SANCTUARY DREAMS

The night sky is clear after the afternoon thunderstorm and water drips from the leafy canopy like a soft rain. It reminds Jack of a long ago summer night on a Virginia farm when he and Mary Lou Simms had taken shelter in her father's hayloft and watched the new moon rising from behind the pale wisps of fleeing storm clouds. The wind had been soft on their faces and there was the sound of distant thunder.

The air had been moist and cool and smelled of honeysuckle and Mary Lou's long blond hair was damp from the rain and strewn with tattered straw. It fell across her face like a golden veil and fluttered gently against her breasts that were wonderful pointed treasures beneath her wet blouse.

"Kiss me Jack" she had breathed in his ear.

He remembers the sound of crickets and the sweet smell of new baled hay and how coarse and exciting it felt against his bare chest and the scent of Mary Lou's lavender soap and the warm moisture of her breasts against his face. He closes his eyes and tries to drown himself in the memory.

There was a final aching sweetness that had been the soft taste of her lips and her face in the moonlight, smiling up at him in wonder and happiness. But then the memory fades and he opens his eyes as an insect hums in his ear. Then he thinks about what has happened.

They had trained in the secrecy of a closed compound at the Air Force base in Udorn Thailand, running ten miles a day in the steaming tropical heat and venturing out into the surrounding country side on live fire patrols that gave them a familiarity with each other under fire. They had been lucky in their one contact with the Pathet Lao rebels. Billy Ray had shot the leader with the Remington on a quick offhand snap shot before they broke contact and the guerillas had melted back into the trees.

"Nice shot Billy Ray" Jack had commented.

Billy Ray smiled like a Cheshire cat.

"We're going to do good boys. I got that lucky feeling."

The team's trainer was an Army Special Forces sergeant they knew only as "Rabbit" He told them his specialty had been sniping and communications but they were going to go over escaping and evading too.

"Now that's not a bad idea" Gunny Robottom had said sarcastically.

He still carried a low opinion of the Army from his days in Korea but grudgingly admitted these Green Berets were a different breed of cat.

"Reckon they would hold the line when the shit comes down" he conceded to the other Marines.

And so they had trained for a month, never knowing more than each other's first name but growing closer day by day. Three days before they were ready to jump off, they went "sterile", which meant no showers, no shaving and no toothpaste.

"Well you boys are getting good and ripe" Gunny Robottom had said with satisfaction.

"You ain't no bouquet of flowers yourself gunny" Billy Ray had said with a smirk.

The team had laughed.

"Yeah, well" the gunny had said sardonically, "The way I smell is gonna be the least of your worries in a few days. And the way you girls smell, the gooks might even think it's one of their own scumbags they're sniffing on the breeze. Lets hope so anyway."

Finally, at the end, Rabbit had pulled Jack aside just before the mission launched.

"Listen Jack, I shouldn't be telling you this but you're a damn good radio operator and I like you and by tonight you guys are gonna be beyond any security worries on our part.

We got an A team over the fence up in Laos. They guard… (And he tells Jack the radio frequency). Listen, I don't like the smell of this op. Too many fucking spooks sniffing around licking their chops. They've already fucked us over a few times. Fucking cowboys and they think they're bullet proof.

If you guys get in the shit, use the call sign "RODENT". I'll tell the A team RTO to listen up for it. Only use it if you are in deep shit.

Those spook motherfuckers hear it and they might try to waste you from the air. Remember, RODENT and listen for an extraction grid."

"Damn Rabbit, thanks! I really appreciate that" says Jack.

"Yeah, well. Good luck Jack. We'll drink some Jack Daniels when you get back."

"Count on it buddy, and thanks."

THE MISSION

That night as dusk began to fall, they had flown north at tree top level and were inserted into the Laotian jungle by a Marine Sikorsky UH-34D "King Bee" helicopter. The helo had been painted a dull black and there were no markings on the sides.

The crew chief, a burly Master Sergeant, seemed more interested in the big Browning fifty caliber machine gun in the doorway then any concern for them or their weight and balance. Then a green light went on in the overhead and he motioned for them to hook up.

The rotor blades changed pitch and then they were hovering over a small clearing faintly visible thirty feet below in the darkness. The team had fast roped out of the helo three at a time as the big helicopter hovered, rocking slightly with the shifting weight as the team disembarked.

When they were on the ground they circled up and waited silently, lying prone in the tall grass as the big Sikorsky eased up into transitional lift and disappeared over the tree tops, its rotor blades making a dull, whopping sound and a faint blue flame flickering from its big round exhaust pipe.

When it was gone and they could hear the night sounds again they moved silently in a single file toward the sanctuary of the dark tree line.

They humped northward for the rest of the night following a fast flowing stream and as the first hazy light of the tropical sun began to warm the humid air, Captain O'Bannion checked his map and pointed to a nearby hill that rose above the surrounding hillsides. He motions Billy Ray forward and points to a spot on the map with an enquiring glance.

Billy Ray had looked at it intently and nodded his head. They had crossed the Laotian border into North Vietnam.

"We're sure as hell in Indian country now sir." Billy Ray said.

"Sure as hell." Obannion agrees.

This is where Intel had said they could make the shot. And for once, it looked like the spooks had gotten it right.

TAKING THE SHOT

The team had hidden themselves on a hilltop overlooking a small village next to a turgid river that was still swollen from the fading monsoon. In the hot morning sun, the water was brown and fast flowing and it carried broken limbs and the swollen bodies of dead animals on its crest.

But the banks were lush and as green as a garden snake and Billy Ray and his spotter position themselves on a small knoll where Billy Ray unwrapped the Remington from its oil soaked sheepskin sheath and rests it upon a firm mound of decayed vegetation. He removed the lens caps from the 3x9 power Redfield scope and placed them in his breast pocket. Then he wrapped a piece of green burlap around the barrel and secured it with green twine. Charlie Dumas, his spotter, uncased his binoculars and scanned the village and then they slowly pulled the green vegetation across their bodies and waited in a zone of strange tranquility like dogs calmed within their crates.

The team is spread in a semi-circle around the shooters several meters away with their rifles pointing outward and they too had covered themselves with vines and leaves. Then they all remained still, and in the hot midday sun, they became invisible along with their thirst.

Billy Ray was twenty one years old and had graduated top of his class at sniper school at Camp Pendleton before transferring to Force Recon. The ammo he was carrying was match grade 30.06 that carried its own unique serial numbers and he had zeroed the rifle carefully and had fired several one inch groups at a thousand yards.

This shot would be slightly longer but the wind was light and directly behind him and the heat shimmer was easy to read from his elevated position above the village. Only Billy Ray and Captain O'Bannion knew the true identity of the target. Billy Ray still couldn't believe it.

Then, in the long, hot afternoon when the urge to sleep became as cruel as thirst, there was movement on the trail below them. Olive green army trucks with the red star of the North Vietnamese army painted on their sides began arriving in a long convoy.

Most of the trucks carried NVA soldiers and they jumped out and formed up in squads when the trucks came to a stop. Then a green staff car moved around the column and drew up to the village's main structure.

The building was a small Buddhist temple in the center of the village and the car pulled to the pagoda front and stopped. A small Vietnamese man of indeterminate age with a wispy white goatee got out and looked around. He stood with a group of high ranking officers, talking and smoking a cigarette.

He was facing toward Billy Ray and through the scope on its highest power resolution, the face of Ho Chi Minh seemed unnaturally clear in the heat shimmer of the noonday sun.

Billy Ray placed the crosshairs of his scope on the man's chest and began his controlled breathing drill. Finally, he lets out most of his air and holds his breath and focuses on his heartbeat.

Then he begins to caress the Remington's trigger with the faintest beginning of a trigger squeeze. He is deep within the sniper's zone of tranquility and calmness when there is the startled shouting of Vietnamese voices and then the growing blast of automatic weapons.

GOING WRONG

When the NVA security patrol had stumbled across them and the firing started, Jack sees Billy Ray turning to his spotter and shaking his head. He can't make the shot.

"Shit!" Jack thinks. "Now we are really fucked!"

Then they were all firing their M-14s on full auto and trying to move deeper into the underbrush, covering each other with long bursts as they leap-frog past each other, changing magazines as they run.

When they take cover behind a fallen tree, Jack rolls over on his back to reload and an AK-47 round goes through the butt plate of his M-14. It splinters the wooden stock and spalls against the rifle's steel receiver. Shrapnel smashes into his shoulder and the impact of the bullet slams his weapon forward. His left shoulder, wrapped in the rifle sling, dislocates from the impact. But he feels only the impact and little pain although the jacket of his camouflage suit is already soaking with blood.

He will remember later the sharp, adrenalin clouded sound of his M-14's operating rod clicking strangely loud above the ear numbing blasts of outgoing rounds and the green tracers swarming outward like malevolent insects on a blood hunt.

With his right hand he untangles the splintered stock from his wounded arm, pulls his KaBar from its sheath and cuts the sling free. Then he jabs the KaBar into the ground within easy reach and jerks his Colt .45 from its black holster with his right hand.

There is already a round in the chamber and he pulls the hammer back to full cock with his thumb, flips the safety off and eases his finger onto the trigger. His left arm is numb and slippery with blood but there is little pain and he forces himself to focus.

He lies on his back against the radio, his feet toward the enemy and the pistol is braced across his blood soaked arm pointing outward between his boots.

An NVA solider in a green, sweat stained uniform and a leaf covered pith helmet breaks from cover and charges towards him his Ak-47 on his hip, firing on full auto.

The green tracers are going overhead and snapping into the trees behind him with a vicious, cracking sound. This close the bullets are supersonic and are breaking the sound barrier as they pass over his head.

Jack holds the pistol with his good hand and steadies it across his damaged arm. He is lying flat on his back now, his head and shoulders straining forward, his boots forming a wide dark V, and the NVA looks like a dancing puppet between them. He extends his arm and raises the pistol and fires.

In the haze of battle and adrenalin and trick of light, he actually sees the bullet as a flick of fat, metallic copper as it arcs over and hits the NVA in the chest.

The 230 grain metal jacketed slug is traveling at 860 feet per second but to Jack's adrenalin swollen eyes it seems to float downwards like a big league curveball. It smacks into the NVA's chest with the impact of one ton of kinetic energy and the small Vietnamese solider is lifted from his feet and slammed backwards with amazing force. His helmet flies off and he hits the ground and lays quivering with his arms spread out to each side as though in final supplication.

A fountain of blood is gushing from his chest, and to Jack, in the dream-like state of battle, the blood seems delicate and slowly blossoming in the sunlight like a Christmas poinsettia.

All these things seem slow and clear and bright to Jack while they are happening and in later years he will play them back in his mind over and over again like an erotic scene in a surrealistic movie that goes on and on.

When he realizes the NVA is down, Jack takes a deep breath and holds the pistol next to his leg. The adrenalin continues to consume him and there is still little pain from his wound, but his body is shaking badly.

He raises the pistol up again and fires at the muzzle flashes in the nearby undergrowth.

"Return fire" Jack says to himself like a mantra.

"Return fire. Return fire."

And then, absurdly, Hamlet speaks to him… "To be or not to be…"

Time passes into itself and there is only sound and movement and bright throbbing color and eventually a great thirst.

And then they are on the run.

ON THE RUN

"Rally point! Rally point!" Captain O'Bannion shouted. The team fanned out, firing on full auto and leapfrogging past each other, dropping a full magazine by Carl Torger the team's tail end Charlie, as they passed.

"Rally point!" The team shouted to each other as they disappeared into the green darkness.

The Gunny and Carl Torger sprayed the oncoming NVA with automatic fire, Torger's M-14 hurling green tracers on the oncoming NVA, knocking them down like bowling pins and the Gunny's Thomson gun ejecting brass into the air in a steady stream, it's barrel smoking from the continuous muzzle blast.

The NVA wavered under the hail of fire and melted back into the dense green undergrowth.

"Go Carl!" the Gunny shouted.

Torger emptied his M-14, jammed in a fresh magazine and picked up the full magazines by his feet. He stuffed them into his rucksack and ran for the nearby tree line. Robottom glanced over his shoulder to make sure he was gone then emptied his Thompson gun at the NVA's muzzle flashes across the clearing. Then he too turned and sprinted for the covering undergrowth.

They came in cautiously, one by one, to the rally point in a thicket of bamboo overlooking a fast flowing river and spread out in a semicircle facing the trail, their weapons at the ready. The camouflage paint on their faces is streaked with sweat and their eyes are wide with adrenalin and exhaustion.

The wounded grimaced in silence. Jack gasped for breath, stumbling under the weight of the radio, the loss of blood beginning to cloud his vision. He crawled the last few yards and sank to the ground beside Captain O'Bannion.

"Good man Jack" O'Bannion says softly.

Jack nods and puffs his cheeks out, expelling his breath in long wracking gasps.

When Torger and the Gunny slide into the thicket, the team circles up and count heads. Torger says, "That fucking tracker they got on point is good. I laid a false trail but it's not gonna fool him for long. Maybe ten minutes at the most."

O'Bannion nods. "I wanted to avoid this but we're gonna have to take him down. And quietly. The rest of those fuckers will be at least a half hour behind him. It'll give us some breathing room."

The team thinks about this. They know it is high risk. A shot or a shout would be a beacon for the NVA to home in on. But they have no other choice. The tracker is too close. The Gunny takes off the green sweat stained bandana from his head and wipes sweat from the stubble of his short gray hair and nods in agreement.

O'Bannion turns to Billy Ray and says, "Use the Hush Puppy. Make it a clean head shot. Let him get in close."

"Roger that skipper" Billy Ray says and pulls the 9 millimeter Browning Hi Power pistol from his rucksack.

The barrel is threaded and Billy Ray screws on a six inch suppressor, releases the magazine and carefully strips and then reloads the subsonic rounds.

Their powder load is calibrated to reduce the bullet's velocity below the speed of sound so there is no sonic crack of the round breaking the sound barrier. This and the suppressor that controls the sound of expanding gasses when the weapon is fired produces only a sharp pop and the click of the pistol's slide cycling back and forth.

It was an ideal weapon for silently neutralizing enemy guard dogs, hence its nickname, 'Hush Puppy'. But now, Billy Ray was going to use it to kill a man.

The team knows that the tracker will be following one of their trails that all come together at the rally point so they set the ambush in the bamboo thicket.

They lie prone, spread in a semi-circle, waiting, silent and invisible in the stifling heat.

THE AMBUSH

The tracker seems to just suddenly appear. One moment there is only the dense green tree line. Then he is there, a small, gaunt man with taut, sun darkened skin stretched over high cheekbones. His movements are slow and flowing like a snake's as he pauses to examine the undergrowth. He sees something and slowly drops to one knee and holds his AK-47 in one hand, its butt on the ground.

Billy Ray carefully raises the Hush Puppy and braces it across his left forearm. The tracker is close and Billy Ray can see that he has buck teeth and a ragged scar across his cheek. He slowly lets the pistol sights drift onto the man's head and starts to gently squeeze the trigger.

The NVA, whose name was Hi Son, feels his warrior's sixth sense begin to tickle the hair on his neck. He starts to throw himself prone just as Billy Ray fires.

Somewhere, in a land far away, a butterfly's wing brushes a rose petal and the universe realigns. The slow moving bullet only chips the tracker's chinbone in a splatter of blood and flies on. Hi Son drops as though pole axed and lies still.

"Fuck!" Billy Ray curses silently.

The team looks at each other in astonishment and gathers around the fallen NVA.

"Well that was one hell of a shot Billy Ray" Captain O'Bannion says sarcastically. "Too bad we don't need a prisoner."

Billy Ray looks down at the man with a sheepish look.

"This fucker sure had good reflexes" he muses.

O'Bannion and the Gunny are already going through Hi Son's small back pack. They discard a small bag of rice and riffle through some papers. A small packet falls out and they open it. There are some strips of ribbons that looks like combat decorations. And a miniature picture of a small, slender woman holding a baby to her breast.

"Must be his wife the Gunny grunts. And from the looks of these ribbons he must be one hardcore son of a bitch."

Jack looks at the picture of the mother and child and something tightens in his throat.

The NVA begins to stir, then comes awake, blood oozing from his shattered chin, the white bone showing. The Gunny places his knee on the tracker's chest. Comprehension floods the man's eyes. Then hatred. He shakes his head back and forth and struggles to sit up. But the Gunny is too heavy for him and he sinks back resignedly.

O'Bannion stuffs the papers into his jacket, looks at the Gunny and nods his head. Robottom looks at him for a long moment then nods back. He shifts his weight slightly and with a strange, tender gesture of respect, slides one hand over Hi Son's eyes, leans over and kisses him on the forehead.

Then, in one fluid movement, he draws his Ka-Bar and cuts Hi Son's throat.

Jack watches in disbelieve. Then revulsion. He knows the Gunny had been on Guadalcanal where the Marines had met the Japanese savagery without mercy and in kind, cutting gold teeth from still living Japanese.

"So that's what it's like." Jack thinks involuntarily.

He feels numb, the pain of his wound forgotten. There is a gurgling sound and a throb of blood and Hi Son's body jerks spasmodically as the blood gushes onto his sweat stained chest.

Finally, after what seemed a long time to Jack, he lies still.

Gunny Robottom points to Doc Walker and Carl Torger and nods towards the river. The men each take an arm and drag the body out into the stream. Blood streams in long ropey coils on the fast flowing water and in the hot sunlight undulates like thin red water snakes as it dissipates.

Robottom steadies the body with one hand, and then gives it a gentle nudge. The current catches it and it drifts away down stream. He looks at it for a long moment and then raises his hand in a slow salute.

"Let's move" O'Bannion orders.

The team checks their weapons and moves downstream in single file towards the south as the hot afternoon sun bakes down on their heads and the trees on the river bank cast undulating shadows on the flowing water that looks like the green venom of a poisonous snake, merciless, cunning and eternally patient, waiting in ambush.

IN THE DARKNESS OF A WARM NIGHT

The men are silent and resting and taking comfort in their own thoughts and there is only the gurgling sound of the river and the night sounds of animals and the rustling of the wind.

The green camouflage paint on their faces is smeared and darkened by burnt cordite from their fired weapons and streaked with sweat and river water and the stubble of their beards lies like a coarse mask on their faces. When they look skyward, the whites of their eyes seem to shine in the moonlight with a strange and terrible innocence.

THE WABASH CANNONBALL

High above them, a Boeing B-52 Stratofortress and her two sister ships flee southward. The three plane cell is spread in a staggered formation a quarter mile apart and in the night sky they are like dark swans against the full moon, their long contrails streaming behind them in long, white combs, virginal in the moonlight. To the watching Marines, they seem magical and otherworldly and as far away from home as they are.

Then there is a new sound and the men come alert as one organism. A distant roaring becomes an F-4 Phantom recon jet in camouflage paint, her twin exhaust plumes a pale yellow trailing dark smoke.

She thunders over their heads at five hundred feet and they catch a fleeting glimpse of a bold logo on the fuselage… MARINES. And then it is gone.

"Well well" says the Gunny. "They even got the air dales over here already."

The Phantom disappears over a distant ridgeline and is gone. Then, as the men start to relax, there is dull boom and a flash of light. The Phantom is coming back on a crescendo of thunder, climbing out into the night sky, her twin afterburners streaming hot orange flame. She is accelerating and climbing and seconds later the team sees the burning exhaust of a surface to air missile closing on her trail. As they watch open mouthed the missile locks on and begins to gain on the fleeing jet.

"Oh Shit" Charlie Dumas says. "The bogey man is going to get him."

Then, when the Phantom's fate seems decided, the gods of war in their eternal perversity decide to roll a pair of snake eyes for the NVA gunners and the missile booster burns out.

The Phantom crew seems to know this and as the ship goes supersonic the pilot pulls the hurtling jet into a vertical climb. And there, over the dark, trackless wilderness, a long way from home, he does a slow roll.

"Goddamn!" Billy Ray says as the sonic boom rolls over them like Promethium thunder. "Did you see that?!" "I swear I saw the back seater give Charlie the finger!"

"Well one thing for sure" Jack says. "We got to be the only round eyes in the world that saw that happen! I feel sorry for those abed this good evening when they could be out here with us enjoying life."

"I'd love to buy those guys a drink someday" Captain O'Bannion muses.

That wasn't something you see every day."

"Yeah skipper, a regular fuckin airshow" the Gunny says.

The team stifles a laugh and goes back to its watchfulness.

STARLIGHT DREAMS

The men lie back against the river bank and look at the stars and think how wonderful it would be to smoke a cigarette but they know the smell of tobacco on the wind would be like spilling blood in shark infested water and they add it to the other things they are missing as they watch the B-52s move serenely against the black vault of eternity and the Phantom's afterburners flicker out and she is gone like fading thunder in the dark night.

Billy Ray nudges his spotter who nods and then props his M-14 with its Starlight night scope on top of the river bank and scans the darkness again. "Nothing" he whispers. Billy Ray nods and cradles the Remington in his arms and rolls over on his back and rests his head against the river bank.

He has fired all the extra 30-06 boat tail rounds that he carried in the band of his boonie hat and the hat's soft brim that Billy has rolled upward on the front and back crushes against the river bank. He feels the warm mud squish against his neck with a soft, comforting texture and he reaches into his rucksack and feels around for the extra ammo.

He grabs a fistful of extra rounds and without looking, pushes them one by one into the looped band of his boonie hat, their slugs pointing upward. Their weight gives him a powerful, satisfied feeling as though he is wearing a crown.

The river mud smells of decaying vegetation and not at all like the clean, salty smell of the oyster beds back home. But the texture is comforting and when he closes his eyes, the gurgling water and the smell of strange flowers is comforting and he thinks about a girl he knew in high school a thousand years ago. Then his eyes flutter and he sinks into a deep sleep and into the land of dreams where she is waiting for him.

BILLY RAY'S DREAM

After they had done all that teenagers could do in the rumble seat of a hot rod '32 Ford roadster on a warm summer night parked on a deserted country lane in rural America, Billy had unbuttoned her blouse and shyly moved his hand inside the clinging silk with an awkward, tentative motion.

He felt like he was trespassing in Shangri La and expected her to say please don't like other girls. But Christine had just wriggled closer to him and placed her hand over his and helped him push it underneath her bra.

Then she licked the inside of his ear with her tongue and bit the tender lobe with her sharp white teeth and had drawn blood. And then she whispered in a low, hoarse voice,

"Make love to me Billy."

It was the summer of 1957, the Golden Age of America, and they were both virgins and her words made his heart stop with fear and longing and a choking excitement. Later he thinks it was almost like the first few milliseconds after you get hit by a bullet. There isn't a lot of pain, just a profound sense of shock. And years later, looking back, he remembers both of these feelings and is still amazed at their power.

He remembers her teasing him about how long it had taken him to unhook her bra (her "undershirt" she had joked) and then there was the startling fullness of her breasts that were suddenly free and pale and wonderfully large, swaying in the moonlight like naked dancers in an ice age garden.

For a long instant of time he couldn't breathe because her breasts seemed so exquisite and unexpected and so far beyond his fantasies that, (had he known the words) he would have believed they could only have come from the imagination of God.

Then they were sitting on the old Army blanket he has taken from the rumble seat and listening to "One Summer Night" on the radio and they are surrounded by lightning bugs that blink softly in the night.

Their bodies glistened in the moonlight with a fine sheen of perspiration and Christine was rocking gently back and forth on the blanket with her eyes closed and her head thrown back to the summer night. Her blond hair fell softly across her face in the moonlight like a gossamer veil and the palms of her hands were flat against the ground and she seemed to be in a place far away, listening to music.

Her breasts sway gently with the motion of her rocking, the nipples dark and erect and Billy couldn't take his eyes off of them. He knew without thinking that he was a humble acolyte at an eternal altar. So he reached over awkwardly with both hands and stroked them with a tender reverence and when he felt the nipples harden beneath his fingers his heart skips another beat.

This too was a wonderful mystery and he took off his shirt and lies back on the blanket and remembers how gracefully she lies back next to him, her bare shoulder touching his, kicking off her sandals, one at a time, flipping them over her head with a slow, theatrical gesture and how her toe nails were the color of dark blood in the moonlight and how the faint scent of her perfume had made his heart race.

"Oh Billy Ray…" she had whispered softly.

She turned her body to him and held him closely in her arms, her breasts warm against his chest, and kissed him with an urgent, tender passion.

Afterward, when he tried to speak, she held her hand to his mouth and kissed him so sweetly he found his eyes were wet with tears.

"I love you" he had said desperately.

"I love you too" she had replied.

But they meant different things, and only their innocence was true and it only because they had shared in its passing.

CROSSINGS

"How's it going Jack?" O'Bannion whispers.
"Keepin on goin Skipper"

"Let's give it one more shot with the Angry Nine. If we don't make contact we'll dump it in the river. That generator is too fucking heavy to keep on carrying."

"Roger that sir" Jack said. "I was thinking the same thing myself."

Jack rubbed his wounded shoulder. It hurt like hell now even though Doc Walker had noticed the dislocation after he cleaned the wound and he had reset it by placing his foot in Jack's armpit and rotating the arm outward. There had been an audible pop as the shoulder joint realigned and then Jack felt an easing of the separate pain of the dislocation.

The corpsman had strapped Jack's arm across his chest, explaining that the joint was so tender and weak now that it was all but useless anyway. He gave Jack one sterette of morphine to take the edge off and what Jack remembered later was that the pain was still there but the morphine feeling was so much better he didn't care about the other pain.

"How's the pain, Jack?" Doc had asked.

"'Tis not so deep as a well, nor so wide as a church door; but 'tis enough'." Jack had replied with a grin.

"You sound like Shakespeare Jack." Doc had laughed.

"Romeo and Juliet my man, Romeo and Juliet."

"Looks like you are gonna have to do some fancy juggling between the radio and your .45"

"Thanks Doc. Appreciate it".

Jack turned to O'Bannion and said, "Skipper we should probably string the long wire antenna as high up and as long as possible. Run it east to west for the best radiation pattern. The gooks will hear it but so will that A team—I hope."

O'Bannion nodded, then turned and spoke in a low voice to Carl Torger. "Take this long wire down trail as far as it will go and string it up a tree as far up as you can reach. String it east to west." Torger nodded and disappeared in the darkness. When he came back, he gave Jack a thumbs up and resumed his watch as the team's tail end Charlie.

Jack hooked the antenna wire to his transmitter and nodded at the man carrying the small tripod mounted generator and the man starts cranking the twin handles of the generator that looks like an oversized coffee grinder.

Jack tunes the transmitter section and as the side tone comes up in his earphones he sends the letters ZZZ three times indicating a Flash Urgent message to follow. Then he sends the three, five letter code groups that gives their identifier and urgent need for help, and then, in plain language, RODENT.

He listens intently after every sequence but there is only the sound of mocking static and the crash of distant lightning.

ELECTRONIC WARRIORS

High above them in the windowless electronic warfare bay of the lead B-52 named The Wabash Cannonball, the Electronic Warfare Officer, Captain Tommy Bolan, hears the Marine radio operator on one of his guard frequencies.

Bolan knows the North Vietnamese still use Morse code and sometimes it will give him an early warning that a missile site is preparing to fire so he has made it a habit to tune one of his standby radios to scan the lower frequencies. But now he realizes that the hand keyed Morse is in English and it is not hard for him to copy it at this slow speed.

The code groups are meaningless to him but he knows that this far north it can only be what it actually is and he can imagine the hard, desperate situation the Marines must be facing by the deliberate, urgent tempo of the radio operator's sending.

He would like to respond but his single sideband transmitter won't load in the CW mode on that low a frequency and he doesn't know if the men below him are listening on a voice channel. So Captain Bolan closes his eyes for a second and thinks, "Good luck boys." He copies the time and frequency in his log and relays the message to Udorn on his command channel radio.

He is turning back to his radar scope when his intercom overrides the radio and he hears his tail gunner, Chief Master Sergeant James J. Kearny calling in an urgent voice.

"Captain! Heads up! SAMS 6 o'clock low!"

Kearny, from the windows of his tail gun compartment, has seen the launch of surface to air missiles five miles below him.

The B-52 tail gunners had often joked that they had the ultimate box seats from which to watch the end of the world—an allusion to nuclear Armageddon. But now they were bombing peasants in the jungle and Armageddon had detached itself from the earth and was lifting skyward like a swarm of flaming onions.

At first they are only rising balls of fire. Then the missiles themselves become black telephone poles with fiery tails.

"Roger Sarge" Bolan responds. "I've got them."

Captain Bolan watches the swarms of surface to air missiles rising on his radar scope and he feels a cold premonition. It is Death approaching on tails of orange fire. In the green flickering darkness of the electronic warfare bay the blips seem as innocent as a swarm of fireflies on a summer night. But Captain Tommy is not new to this game. And he is under no illusions.

"How many you count Sarge?"

"Looks like about fifteen or twenty at launch sir. Coming from different sites. They're barraging us. I count at least seven starting to home on us" Kearny reports.

Bolan looks at his equipment and sees that the missile's radar guidance uplink is active. He toggles a switch that fires a thunderbolt of invisible lightning as deadly as a shotgun. It jams the uplink signal and the missiles guidance system breaks lock.

Some of the fireflies arc away and then detonate as harmless as skyrockets over the Washington monument on the Fourth of July. But each missile guides on its own frequency and there are too many of them for even the B-52's powerful electronic weapons.

Four of the missiles are not spoofed and close on the gallant, doomed bomber as she thunders along at thirty thousand feet, majestic and defiant in the cold pristine air, her long ghostly contrails ethereal in the moonlight.

The Wabash Cannonball's two sister ships spread miles apart on either side as the SAMS launch, only their navigation lights visible in the humid night. They have their own worries. They too are being hunted by the enemy's relentless birds of prey.

"I've got active uplink" Bolan radios the other planes.

"Roger Cannonball, we've got it. Going to ECM now."

The SAMs are not high tech. But they fly faster than the speed of sound and they come on like suicidal sharks on a blood trail. In their electronic brains they are focused and single minded. They will do as their electron master commands.

But it comes down to knowledge, experience and energy. Captain Bolan is better than the North Vietnamese SAM shooters he is dueling with. His electronic weapons can defeat many of the missiles but not all. Bolan knows there are no guarantees in combat and the enemy electronic warriors know this applies to them also.

Bolan wishes he had some of the new F-105 Wild Weasels in the area to take out the Sam sites. Their Shrike AGM missiles would ride the uplink signal down to the launch site and destroy it. But he doesn't and the cosmic dice of war are tumbling as they fall.

Sergeant Kearny also knows that the immutable laws of physics and math do not favor them this night. There are just too many of them coming up.

"Fucking flying telephone poles" thinks Jim Kearny bitterly. "What a way to go after thirty years in this business."

Kearny is on his last combat mission, a three war veteran and a legend in the Air Force. He had to call in some favors to get assigned to the Cannonball. But there was a special reason he wanted her. She was one of the early model B-52s, the version that still had a tail gun position that placed the gunner in the same compartment with his gun just like a world war two bomber.

In addition, the Cannonball's four fifty caliber machine guns had been replaced by the new experimental 6 barrel 20 mm Vulcan cannon for testing under combat conditions.

The gun could link to the fire control radar and had a spectacular 4000 round a minute rate of fire and a four thousand yard range—twice that of the fifty cals. Kearny was impressed.

"Wish we had this boy in the old days" he thought. "Bye bye Fw-190s and Mig-15s". Kearny thought the Cannonball was a fitting place for his final mission.

He breathes deeply in his oxygen mask and his mind drifts back to 1950 and he is high over the Chosin Reservoir in Korea at the tail gun of a B-29 watching the First Marine Division fight its way to the sea.

The Marines were outnumbered ten to one and they carry their dead and wounded with them. But they destroy eight Chinese divisions and the magnificence of their fighting withdrawal passes into legend. To have been at "The Frozen Chosin" marked a man for life.

Kearny remembers firing his twin fifties at the massing Chinese far below. It made him feel like he was helping the Marines. "Semper Fi boys" he says softly. And he meant it. His kid brother Timmy was down there.

Later, he drank with him in Tokyo. And Kearny felt shocked to realize that his brother was still a teenager except that now he seemed to have the face of an old man and his hair had turned white.

His skin was still pale and gaunt from the sleepless, frozen nights and hours of brutal combat and it was stretched tautly across the deep hollows of his checks. But it was his eyes that worried Kearny the most. They seemed as dark and pitiless as an empty grave.

In the brutal nights of bombing that followed the Chosin, when the B-29s suffered badly, Kearny remembers firing his twin fifties at the darting Migs that streamed southward in long deadly ghost trains over the frozen Yalu River, silhouetted against the full moon like killer birds.

They were so fast it was hard to lead them. His Browning fifty calibers were wonderful, but only to a thousand yards. Then gravity took over and it was like spraying a garden hose at night flying bats.

SUZANNE

Now time has slowed as it often does in combat and a part of Kearny's mind continues to drift. It is 1943 and he is eighteen again and a waist gunner in a Boeing B-17 Flying Fortress named Suzanne.

The bomber is named after the pilot's girlfriend, a voluptuous English redhead with green eyes, and she is painted provocatively with parted thighs across both sides of the bomber's nose. Beneath her long, outstretched legs, her name is a sexy signature—*SUZANNE.*

But young Jim Kearny is not thinking about the pilot's girlfriend. He is tracking the quick twisting FW 190s that are swarming around his squadron, snapping short bursts from his single fifty caliber Browning machine gun.

The air is forty below zero as it roars through the open waist gun window but sweat forms beneath his electrically heated suit and puddles in the slick interior of the rubber expansion bulb of his oxygen mask.

He swings the heavy gun in quick, urgent arcs, his fleece gloved fingers on the twin triggers, and his perfect, eighteen year-old 20/10 eyes are wide open and concentrating behind their thick high altitude goggles.

The bomber's deck is littered with spent shell casings and the frozen blood of the other waist gunner who has lost an arm to a 20 millimeter shell. For some reason the round hadn't exploded. It simply tore off the man's arm and then exited through the plane's fuselage. Now the arm is frozen in a pool of dark blood on the plane's metal deck like a piece of macabre sculpture.

The gunner is not yet dead, but unconscious and slumped over his gun like a rag doll. His other arm is locked around the gun and his body sways with an odd dignity to the motion of the airplane.

The freezing air has mercifully staunched the flow of blood and Kearny thinks that if the fighters break off in time he can leave his gun and may be able to get a tourniquet around the stump.

But Suzanne is still under attack and badly wounded. Cold sunlight streams through the dozens of holes made by the German machine gun and cannon fire and one engine is smoking.

Suzanne's pilot is dead from the same 88 millimeter round that exploded over the cockpit and killed the radio operator and the top gunner. The copilot has feathered the propeller and regains control. But Suzanne is streaming fuel and they have miles to go across the English Channel.

On the bottom of the airplane the belly turret is a shattered mass of twisted aluminum and shards of Plexiglas that are smeared with red gore. In the howling slipstream the splinters of Plexiglas snap like frozen pennants.

The ball turret has taken a direct hit from a 30 millimeter cannon shell fired by one of the new ME-262 jet fighters that has risen vertically from the green German farmland on twin jets of yellow flame, its four, thirty millimeter cannon flickering deadly flames. Suzanne's belly gunner sees him coming and spins the Bendix turret around on a dime and depresses his twin fifties downwards to face the rising fighter.

But just as he presses his triggers, a cannon shell from the rocketing Messerschmitt blows through the bullet proof Plexiglas and detonates against his chest.

In the tight confines of the ball turret, nineteen year old Willy Johanson from Clearlake Minnesota sees only a flash of light before his body explodes. In the macabre roulette of war, Willy's left arm, is blown through the turret's shattered hatch and comes to rest between the feet of the dead radio operator whose lifeless eyes seem to stare at it in mild rebuke.

When Suzanne lets down through the warm summer air of England, the small ponds of frozen blood in her bullet riddled body thaw quickly and the waiting medics see it streaming from the seine of bullet holes along the plane's bottom in shades of primary red. When they board, the blood is deep and slippery and Willy's arm floats free from the dead radio operator and slides gently along to the rear where it bumps into Kearny's foot and comes to rest along side the other waist gunner's missing arm.

SARGEANT KEARNEY'S LAST STAND

These memories flit by on a dark wave and are gone. And then that old familiar feeling of being far from home takes its place and Jim Kearny thinks it is the loneliest feeling in the world. He wants to fire back but now there are no

MIGS or FW 190s to shoot at. No enemy warriors. Only soulless predators with fiery tails and electronic nostrils that follow the Cannonball's invisible radio scent through the twisting canyons of cloud and monsoon mist.

The only men firing at each other are Captain Bolan and the S a.m. operators somewhere far below in the brooding darkness. And their weapons are too silent and swift and deadly to be honored by an old warrior. And yet they can kill.

Then Kearny sees the moonlight flicker on the dull green paint of the nearest missile that is closing on them and Chief Master Sergeant Jimmy Kearny figures; "What the hell." Ignoring his radar sight, he raises the gun to maximum elevation and holds the trigger down.

The six barrels of the 20 millimeter Vulcan cannon rotate like a buzz saw and hurl explosive shells out at 4000 rounds a minute. For Jim Kearny it has all come down to the same Kentucky windage used by riflemen on the American frontier two hundred years before.

Kearny, his blue eyes still as sharp as a fighter pilot's, raises the gun ever so slightly and watches the shells cast a graceful sparkling arc like a garden hose full of fireflies. And then one of them, at the extreme limit of its range, like an improbable karmic consolation prize tossed down from Valhalla by the gods of war, strikes an oncoming missile and it explodes in an orange and black fireball.

"Fuck you" shouts Chief Master Sergeant James Kearny, his finger still on the trigger and his warrior's blood rising.

He hunts for another target, his cannon shells spraying across the night sky, and for a split second he sees the red star on another rocket deflecting clear, spoofed by the last of Bolan's ECM pulse. "And fuck you too" he hisses.

He has fired the last of his 7,000 round supply and his empty cannon barrels are still spinning as the missile arcs over and detonates harmlessly a mile away. Jim Kearny snaps a final, silent salute to his comrade in the ECM bay who has scored with his last dying burst of electronic energy.

Then he pulls off his oxygen mask and reaches into his flight jacket and takes out a cigarette. He lights it, inhales deeply and closes his eyes. Then he bows his head in prayer.

The last two missiles hit the fleeing bomber and she shudders as one wing folds upward in a blazing funeral pyre of burning jet fuel. Then the Wabash Cannonball nods once with a slow, stately dignity and starts her long lonely spiral into the dark night far below.

The resting Marines cheer silently as they watch Sergeant Kearny's last stand at 30,000 feet. Even at that distance, they can see the tiny silver specks of his cannon fire arcing gracefully against the night sky. And they recognize a brother warrior fighting against impossible odds.

When the Wabash Cannonball staggers from the exploding missiles, the team grimaces and watches intently for parachutes. But there are none and they bow their heads in silent tribute.

"Hell of a gunner" Billy Ray says.

Then the team mounts up and resumes its long, desperate march southward through the moonlit darkness as bits of smoking wreckage begin to fall around them.

BENEDICTION

Jack's eyes flutter open and as they focus he sees a figure in white. Jack thinks it is an angel. "Heaven?" he wonders through the morphine haze.

The Angel takes his good hand and squeezes it.

"Welcome back corporal" the Angel says

"Where...where am I?" Jack asks.

"Base hospital in Udorn" the Angel says in the sweetest voice Jack has ever heard. "You've had a rough time."

Jack's head clears and he remembers.

"What about my team?" he asks, his throat so dry he can barely croak out the words.

The Angel, who is an Air Force nurse and too young for this place, places her other hand on his and pats it.

"I'm sorry Jack," she says gently, tears welling in her eyes, "Your chopper crashed on the runway... and there was a fire. Only you and Corporal Wallace made it out. I know its no consolation she lied, but they were all dead before the fire. Even the pilot. He must have had just enough left to set her down.

THE EXTRACTION

Jack tries to think about this and then remembers the NVA trackers catching them at the extraction site and how they had all been hit as they fled for the black King Bee helo, firing and leapfrogging, Billy Ray kneeling and aiming, his Remington cracking with deadly accuracy. And how Captain O'Bannion and Gunny Robottom had stood side by side, firing their weapons and covering them as they scrambled aboard the hovering helo, the Gunny's Thompson gun ejecting brass in a glittering arc over O'Bannion's head and the skipper, kneeling and firing his M-14 on full auto, spraying the tree line and changing magazines as the team dragged each other onboard.

When the Gunny went down, O'Bannion had grabbed him with one magnificent linebacker's arm and flung him into the helo and turned back and fired his last magazine at the oncoming NVA as the helo started to lift off.

Then there had been a deep rumbling sound and two Marine A-1 Sky Raiders called in by the King Bee pilot appear across the tree line. Their 2500 HP R-3350 Wright radial engines were roaring behind the whirling blur of their big four bladed propellers and their four 20 millimeter cannon are coughing yellow flames with a rapid thumping sound.

The planes were so low their props are snapping high hanging tree branches as they bore in. The NVA caught in the open were burst apart in clouds of flying body parts and red mist as the explosive rounds hit them.

Then the planes rolled knife edge to the ground and pulled around in a 6 G turn, white contrails streaming from their wing tips. They were fifty feet off the ground and the wings were shuddering on the edge of an accelerated stall as they came around for another pass.

Jack remembers a fleeting moment of profound love for the Marine aviators who were pushing so far beyond safe limits for the sake of their brother Marines on the ground.

Then he was ducking under the door gunner who is ankle deep in fifty caliber shell casings and still firing through a red hot barrel at the oncoming NVA. He grabbed the skipper's wrist with his good arm and is pulling with all his strength as the King Bee shuddered from the impact of incoming rounds as she lifted off.

Just as it seemed O'bannion would make it, an AK round punched through his body between the shoulder blades and for a long instant that Jack will never forget, their eyes met. O'Bannon seemed to smile faintly and mouth the words… Semper Fi. But Jack couldn't be sure and then the light went out of O'Bannion's eyes and he fell forward into the chopper, his head coming to rest on Jack's chest and his blood soaking though to Jack's skin like a warm absolution. Then they were lifting away from the green hell of the jungle, trailing shell casings and a mist of hydraulic fluid and blood like an unholy benediction of bitter farewell.

And then, without warning, the memory overwhelms Jack and he starts sobbing and it feels like a hot claw is tearing fistfuls of flesh from his stomach.

The Angel makes a soft shushing sound and with infinite tenderness she wipes his brow. "It's going to be ok Jack she says softly. "It's going to be ok."

"Going to be ok" Jack repeats in a fading voice. "Going to be ok…" and he drifts back into the warm darkness where there is no pain.

DEMONS

In the afternoon he awakens and the Angel is still there.

"Hi there" she says brightly. "Feeling a little better?"
"Yeah… I guess so" Jack says tentatively. They look into each others eyes for a long moment but neither speaks.

Then there is a sharp knock on the door and it opens abruptly.

Two men wearing Aloha shirts and sunglasses enter. Jack notices they are both wearing big silver Omega wrist watches. "Hey there Jack!" the fat one says cheerfully. "How's it going?"

Jack just looks at them.

"Who are you and what are you doing in here?" the Angel says sternly. "This is a restricted area."

"I know hon, I know," the fat man says soothingly.

"We just need to ask Jack here a few questions."

"Not until I know who authorized you to come in here" the angel says defiantly.

The smile slid off the fat man's face and he reaches behind him and produces a thin brown billfold. He flips it open and holds it in her face. "This answer your question sweetheart?"

There is no longer any pretense of cordiality in his voice and Jack notices the bulge of a handgun underneath the man's red and green Aloha shirt. The other man, slim and athletic looking has said nothing but his eyes keep moving around the room as though memorizing everything in sight.

"I'll have to get the colonel." She says defiantly.

"You do that honey" the fat man snarled, "and close the door on your way out."

The Angel gives Jack a reassuring pat and backs slowly out of the room. The fat man pulls a chair next to Jack's bed and rests his chin on his fists and looks at Jack for a long time.

"You know who we are Jack?"

"Yeah" Jack says warily. "I recognize the sunglasses."

He is starting to get a cold feeling in his stomach and his wounds are throbbing.

"Yeah, sure you do Jack."

"Well, what do you want?" Jack says.

The fat man leans closer until his face is only inches from Jack's and in a cold voice says, "You boys fucked up Jack. Your buddy Billy Ray didn't make the shot did he?"

"We got in a firefight..." Jack starts to explain. Then stops when he sees that this doesn't make any difference to the fat man.

"Fucked up big time Jack. And we can't have fuck ups running around talking to the press can we Jack?"

Jack starts to feel the first faint tendrils of fear creeping through his body. He wishes he had a weapon. Irrationally, he thinks, "Maybe the Angel can bring me my .45."

"What are we going to do with you Jack? You and Billy Ray?" the fat man says in reasonable tone of voice as though he were a manager discussing options with a baseball pitcher who has just walked three guys in a World Series game.

Jack says nothing and steals a look at the other Aloha shirt that is standing with his back to the corner looking out the window.

Then the door flies open and an Air Force colonel strides into the room.

He is wearing camouflage fatigues with the silver eagles of his rank on his collar, jump wings on his chest, and a Colt .45 in a black shoulder holster. The Angel follows him triumphantly, her large brown eyes lit with an avenging fire.

"I told these men this was a restricted area sir" she said. The colonel nods his head slowly, all the while fixing the fat man with an unblinking stare.

"Want to see my credentials colonel?" the fat man said with barely concealed contempt.

"I know who you are" the colonel said in a measured tone. "The question is, do you know who I am?"

The fat man seemed faintly amused but bitter experience had taught him to take nothing for granted.

"No sir can't rightly say that I do." He said in a conciliatory tone. "I reckon you are the head man around here?"

The colonel's eyes bored into the fat man's face. "Not just around here my friend. Ever hear of…" and he leaned forward and spoke quietly in the fat man's ear.

Jack notices the fat man pale slightly beneath his tan. "You understand sir that we have authority over this mission?" the fat man said in a now respectful manner. "We have to take corporal Phillips with us. As soon as he is able to travel of course." he added in a reasonable tone.

"You don't anymore." the colonel said in a cold voice. "This boy is going back to the states tomorrow. And by the way, he will be escorted by one of my Air Commando teams. Any other questions?"

The fat man looked at his partner and then back at the colonel.

"You sure this is cleared?" the fat man said, now becoming uncertain.

The colonel took a note pad from the table and scribbled a name and phone number on it. He held it up to the fat man's face and said in a quiet, deadly voice, "You recognize this?"

The fat man's eyes bulged slightly.

"Absolutely sir, absolutely. But we have our duties too you know. Tell you what, just let us talk with the corporal for a few minutes alone and we will be on our way."

The Angel looked at her boss in awe.

"You have 10 minutes Mr. Brown. If you are not out of this room by then, you will seriously regret it."

"Thank you sir that will be fine. That will be fine." The colonel looked at the fat man long and hard and slowly nodded his head. "10 minutes."

He turned to Jack and said in a kindly voice, "You hang in there son. You're going home." Then he turned on his heel and strode to the door. He stopped and nodded to the Angel.

"Lieutenant Villareal please wait outside until these gentlemen leave. I assume you are wearing your wristwatch?"

"Yes sir!" the Angel said happily, and followed him from the room.

When the door closed, the fat man, who's ID identified him as Samuel Brown, Studies and Observation Group, walked back to Billy's bedside and stood looking down at him.

"You're one lucky fucker corporal—so far. So let me give you some real good advice. When you get back to the states you just remember you were never here. This mission never existed. And it never will. Your service record will show you spent the last year at Quantico.

I assume you're getting out in September when your enlistment is up. Fine. But if you ever breathe a word about this to anyone you might just end up getting hit by a milk truck on Shirley Highway. Do I make myself clear?"

Jack looked at the corpulent, red veined face and nodded slowly. "I get the picture asshole" he said in a quiet voice, not taking his gaze away from the other man's eyes.

"You better Jack. And if you start to forget, just think about Jack Kennedy."

The fat man nodded to his partner and they moved toward the door.

"One more thing Jack" the fat man said as though with an afterthought.

"Don't even think about putting in for a Purple Heart. And don't let these zoomie assholes around here start writing you up for one either. Understand?"

Jack just stared at him. The fat man turned and they were through the door.

"All yours sweetheart" he snarled at the Angel as they brushed past her. And then they were gone.

The Angel rushed into the room and stood by Jack's bed, the back or her hand against his cheek. "Are you ok Jack?" she asked apprehensively.

"Yeah, yeah, I'm ok" Jack said with a deep sigh.

"I'm glad you're flying out tomorrow Jack. We have a lot of these 'people' coming and going around here lately. It seems like they don't have to answer to anyone and they have a lot of pull. It gives me the creeps."

"Yeah, tell me about it." Jack replies bitterly. "A year ago I was sitting in Quantico with a year to go on my enlistment, loving life. Partying up in D.C. every night, most weekends off. Life was good. Then one day in the motor pool, the First Sergeant says to drive my TRC-75 (that's a radio jeep) up to the Naval Research Lab on the Potomac and report to this Marine colonel.

The colonel takes me in a room and there are these two spooks there that start asking questions. They're wearing sunglasses just like the two assholes that were just in here. What is it with these clowns and sunglasses?

Anyway, they confirmed my background—I had been a radio operator with a top secret clearance in the Marine Comm Detachment aboard the USS Pocono during the Cuban blockade and had been in Force Recon back in '61. And I don't have any family. Guess they figured that about covered all their major food groups. Then they "asked" if I would be willing to "volunteer" for a mission in Southeast Asia. Seemed like a cool idea at the time. Next thing I know I'm on a C-130 bound for here.

I knew things were cranking up. We were testing chopper door guns at Quantico and I remember when I was in radio school back in San Diego in '61, a Marine colonel told us the Corps would be fighting in Laos before the end of the year. Ha. He wasn't far wrong. At least as far as I'm concerned" he said bitterly. Anyway, the next thing I know I'm on my way here. But believe me ma'am you don't want to know any more about the mission."

They were silent for a long time and then the Angel asked,

"What are you going to do when you get out Jack"?

Jack brightens at the thought.

"Going to college mam. Been accepted at American University in D.C. I start in September."

"That's wonderful Jack! You are going to love college. I went to Georgetown myself. D.C. is such a cool place to go to school" she says wistfully.

"What made you pick American?"

"Well mam, when I was at Quantico I used to drink at this bar up on Wisconsin Avenue called The Keg…"

The Angel laughed with delight, her dark brown eyes shinning like warm pools of liquid obsidian.

"Oh God! I know that place!"

"Really!?" Jack says astonished.

"Well, anyway, one night I'm in there with some buds and two jocks are in there wearing their AU letter jackets and they had the two most gorgeous blond college girls I've ever seen. Heard one of them say they were Kappas. Guess that was their sorority? Anyway, right then and there I decided AU was the place for me!"

The Angel laughed delightedly and the sound is like silver against crystal and it makes Jack blush with pleasure.

"Yeah" Jack said wistfully, still not sure it is actually going to happen. "I'm really looking forward to it."

JACK'S SECRET WISH

What Jack is really looking forward to (he admits only to himself) are all those beautiful college girls just waiting for him. And reading Shakespeare and Hemingway and playing the guitar on the quad on one of those soft April afternoons when the lilacs are in bloom and the wind feels like warm perfume against your cheek. And watching the barefoot hippie chicks walk by with their blue toenail polish and no bras on, just those wonderful young tits jiggling under their tie-dyed shirts and peasant blouses.

"Oh man!" Jack thought. "Life is going to be so good." But in his heart he knows it is a prayer that he must keep repeating.

"Sleep now Jack." the Angel says soothingly. "I'm going to put a little more morphine in your drip."

"Thanks ma'am", Jack said. And he closed his eyes.

"To sleep perchance to dream" he murmurs.

And then he is in a place of warmth and peace, and in his dreams Captain O'Bannion comes to him and they embrace.

"Semper Fi Jack," O'Bannion says with infinite sadness.

"Semper Fi Skipper." Jack replies softly, his eyes filling with tears.

O'Bannion smiles wistfully and pats Jack on the shoulder.

"Live a good life Jack" he whispers.

And then he is gone.

FEB 08 2018

CPSIA information can be obtained
at www.ICGtesting.com
Printed in the USA
LVOW10s1521280118
564334LV00011B/286/P